Isaac: A Model of Quiet Leadership

Faithful. Steady. Purposeful.

By Myriam C. Muniz

Independently published

August 2025

Dedication

To the quiet leaders—
The ones who show up, stay faithful, and do the work
even when no one is watching.
This book is for you.

And to my husband Victor,
my rock and greatest encourager,
Thank you for loving me well in every season.

To my daughter Zahra,
Thank you for your sharp eye, soft heart, and steady
support.
You make me better.

And to God—
who sees, who knows, and who rewards faithfulness
done in secret.
All glory belongs to You.

Introduction: A Different Kind of Leader

"You don't have to be flashy to be faithful."
— Myriam Muñiz

When we think of legendary leaders in the Bible, names like Abraham, Moses, David, and Paul immediately come to mind. These were figures of bold action, big miracles, and undeniable charisma. But in the middle of the famous patriarchal trio, Abraham, Isaac, and Jacob, there's someone who led in a quieter way: Isaac.

Isaac didn't see the seas parted like Moses. He didn't wrestle angels like Jacob. His story isn't filled with dramatic speeches or heroic battles. Instead, Isaac's leadership showed up through trust, peace, and obedience. He lived a life of faithful consistency, moving when God told him to move, trusting God for provision, and quietly building a legacy that would outlive him by generations.

This book is for the Isaacs.

It's for the leaders who often feel overlooked — the ones who don't crave the spotlight but still carry influence wherever they go.

It's for the steady hands, the faithful workers, the thoughtful listeners.

It's for the ones who show up, day after day, making a difference in ways that may not always be seen or celebrated.

Maybe that's you.

It was me, too. For a long time, I didn't *feel* like a leader. I preferred to lead from behind the scenes, supporting others, building people up, and doing the work without needing recognition. And yet, people were watching, growing, and being impacted. Just like Isaac, I was leading quietly, consistently, and purposefully, even when I didn't fully realize it.

If you've ever felt like your quiet leadership doesn't matter...

If you've ever wondered if the small faithful steps you take are really making an impact...

I want you to know: **they are**.

Isaac's life proves that leadership isn't always loud. Sometimes the greatest influence comes from a heart fully devoted to God in the ordinary, unseen moments.

In the chapters ahead, we'll look closely at Isaac's story — how he navigated family, faith, waiting, mistakes, and blessings. Along the way, we'll connect his life to leadership lessons, pop culture moments, and biblical truth that can encourage and equip you in your own leadership journey.

Dear Leader, you don't have to be flashy to be faithful. You just have to be willing to walk quietly, consistently, and courageously with God.

Join me by journaling, reflecting, and praying as we walk through Isaac's story.

Let's dive in.

"You are altogether beautiful, my darling; there is no flaw in you."
— Song of Songs 4:7 (NIV)

"The call isn't out there at all — it's inside me."
— *Moana* (Disney's *Moana*)

Chapter 1: You Were Born for This.

Dear Leader,

Have you ever felt like your quiet nature disqualifies you from leadership?
 Like you were placed in the background for a reason and maybe you're supposed to stay there?

If so, you're not alone.

Before we dive deeper into Isaac's story, I want to share a little of my own.

I was born to a single mother who had me later in life, like Sarah, who was in her 90s when Isaac was born. My mom was 38 years old when she had me, a beautiful, unexpected surprise.

We lived a quiet life, just the two of us, and I was always in the background of family and friend groups.

And honestly, that was alright with me.

Even as a child, I was a rule follower, quiet, observant, and obedient.

I didn't seek out the spotlight.
I didn't chase after attention.

Instead, I learned early on that strength could look like listening more than speaking, and that leadership could be modeled through faithfulness, not flashiness.

When I look at Isaac's story, it resonates deeply.

Isaac wasn't born into fame the way his father Abraham was remembered, or into struggle the way his son Jacob was known.

He simply was — steady, faithful, present.
And that was enough.

His life reminds us that leadership isn't always about starting revolutions or commanding crowds.

Sometimes it's about living consistently, quietly, and obediently, exactly how God designed you to be.

Isaac's story reminds us that some of the most powerful lives begin quietly.

After years of waiting, doubting, and even laughing at the possibility, Abraham and Sarah welcomed a son, long after everyone else would have given up hope.

> **Genesis 21:1–3 (NIV)**
> "Now the Lord was gracious to Sarah as he had said, and the Lord did for Sarah what he had promised. Sarah became pregnant

and bore a son to Abraham in his old age,
at the very time God had promised him.
Abraham gave the name Isaac to the son
Sarah bore him..."

Isaac wasn't born out of perfect circumstances.
He was born out of a promise.

His life wasn't random.
It was intentional, crafted by a God who delights in
doing big things in small, quiet ways.

Maybe your life hasn't looked like the movies.
Maybe your story feels small compared to the
highlight reels you see online.

But hear me clearly: **you are no accident.**
You are the fulfillment of dreams, prayers, and
possibilities you can't even see yet.

In pop culture, we often celebrate the loud,
larger-than-life leaders, the ones who are bold, brash,
and center stage.

But there's a different kind of power in listening to the
quiet call within you the way Moana in *Disney's
Moana* hears the ocean's song long before anyone else
believes in her.

At a pivotal moment, Moana realizes, *"The call isn't out there at all. It's inside me."*

She had spent so much time trying to prove herself or earn approval, but the moment of breakthrough came when she accepted the truth about who she already was.

This moment echoes a biblical truth:

Your calling is not about who you're trying to become. It's about who God already says you are.

God has already placed purpose, identity, and power within you through Christ.

Your voice may be quiet. Your steps may be steady. But your calling is divine.

You don't have to chase the call. You carry it.

Dear Leader, if you've ever felt like you're "too quiet" or "too hidden" to make an impact, know this:

You were born for this.

Your steady presence, your faithful obedience, your quiet leadership, they matter more than you know.

Biblical Reflection:

Isaac's life didn't start with a grand entrance.
It started with trust.

The story of Isaac begins long before his birth. His parents, Abraham and Sarah, were promised a child by God, but they waited decades to see that promise fulfilled. Sarah was in her 90s when she gave birth to Isaac. Imagine the level of trust required to keep believing in something that seemed biologically and logically impossible. Every year that passed could have been another reason to stop believing — and yet God's Word prevailed.

Isaac's birth was a miracle, not because his parents were perfect, but because God was faithful. Abraham and Sarah doubted. They laughed. They even tried to "help" God by taking matters into their own hands. But in the end, God kept His promise. Isaac's very existence is a testimony that God's Word never returns void.

This truth is echoed in Psalm 139:

> "For you created my inmost being; you
> knit me together in my mother's womb.
> I praise you because I am fearfully and
> wonderfully made; your works are

wonderful, I know that full well.
 My frame was not hidden from you when I was made in the secret place...
 All the days ordained for me were written in your book before one of them came to be."
 — Psalm 139:13–16 (NIV)

Just as Isaac's life was intentional, so is yours. You are not forgotten. You are not random. **You are designed.** Before anyone saw you, God already knew the days appointed for you. And just like Isaac, your story begins not with perfection, but with trust — trusting that God has placed you here on purpose, for a purpose.

Isaac's beginning shows us that leadership doesn't require a dramatic entrance. You don't need to have it all figured out or live up to the world's standards of success. Your story is proof that God uses ordinary people, born into imperfect circumstances, to carry out extraordinary promises.

What God started in Isaac was far bigger than Isaac himself. It was the continuation of a covenant that would eventually lead to Jesus Christ. And what God has started in you carries purpose far beyond what you can see today.

Leadership Lesson:

Leadership doesn't start when you're handed a title or given a microphone.

It starts when you accept that your life is intentional, that you were placed here for a reason.

You don't need to chase significance.
You already are significant.

You were born for this.

Journal Prompts:

- When was the first time you realized your life had meaning beyond yourself?

- What voices (internal or external) have made you doubt your purpose?

- How would you lead differently if you believed, without a doubt, that you were sent on purpose?

Prayer:

Father,

Thank You for creating me with such care and intention.

Even when I doubt, remind me that I am part of Your promise and Your plan.

Help me walk in confidence, not because of my own strength, but because of Your love that chose me first.

In Jesus' name, Amen.

Chapter 1 Wrap-Up:

You were born on purpose for a purpose.
Like Isaac's miraculous and promised birth, **your existence is not ordinary**. It's marked by divine timing and purpose.

Isaac wasn't born in a hospital or into a perfect nuclear family. He was born to two people who had waited a lifetime and nearly given up. His name literally means "he laughs" because when Sarah heard she'd have a child in her old age, she laughed in disbelief.

God's plans for you were set in motion long before you could imagine them.

You are called.
You are chosen.
You are necessary.

When doubt creeps in, remember:

> "You are altogether beautiful, my darling; there is no flaw in you." *(Song of Songs 4:7 NIV)*

Step boldly into the life God has designed for you.

"Trust in the Lord with all your heart and lean not on your own understanding; in all your ways submit to him, and he will make your paths straight."
— Proverbs 3:5–6 (NIV)

"With great power comes great responsibility."
— Uncle Ben, *Spider-Man* (Marvel)

Chapter 2: "Obedience in the Face of Fear"

Dear Leader,

Some moments stretch us so deeply that obedience feels almost impossible. That's what makes them defining moments; the kind that tests our trust, exposes our fears, and shapes our legacy.

Isaac knew that kind of fear.

The scene in Genesis 22 is heavy.

Abraham has been asked by God to do the unthinkable: offer his son, the very promise he waited a lifetime for, as a sacrifice.

And Isaac? He follows.

When we talk about the story of Abraham offering Isaac on Mount Moriah, we often focus on Abraham's faith. But Isaac wasn't just a passive participant in the story. He was old enough to carry the wood. Old enough to ask the right questions. And old enough to resist, if he wanted to.

> "Abraham took the wood for the burnt offering and placed it on his son Isaac, and he himself carried the fire and the knife. As the two of them went on together, Isaac spoke up and said to his father Abraham, 'Father?'

'Yes, my son?' Abraham replied.

'The fire and wood are here,' Isaac said, 'but where is the lamb for the burnt offering?'

Abraham answered, 'God himself will provide the lamb for the burnt offering, my son.' And the two of them went on together."

— *Genesis 22:6–8 (NIV)*

Imagine the confusion.
Imagine the fear.

There's no record of Isaac putting up a fight. No dramatic monologue or superhero moment.

One of my mentors, **Sue Unvarsky**, often said:

"It's okay to be a little uncomfortable."

Obedience is uncomfortable. It costs something. But in that discomfort, something sacred grows: **trust**.

And here's the truth, obedience may look quiet on the outside, but it moves mountains on the inside.

"With great power comes great responsibility."
— *Uncle Ben, Spider-Man*

If God has called you to lead, lead with trust - quiet, steady, unshakeable trust.

In my early walk with Christ, I remember reading that story and thinking, *"How could Isaac do that?"*

But now I see it differently. I see the strength it takes to trust someone else's obedience to God.

I see the depth of faith required to climb a mountain when you don't fully understand the destination.

I see leadership in Isaac's silence.

Isaac models a quiet strength that isn't loud or flashy, but faithful. His obedience echoes through Scripture, not because of his words, but because of his surrender.

I felt that kind of surrender when my job of over 30 years was eliminated. I didn't see it coming, and I didn't know what to do next. For years, I had poured myself into a career in corporate America and suddenly, it was gone. I was stunned. Hurt. Untethered.

But in the stillness, I heard a whisper in my spirit, not audibly, but undeniably:

"Don't go back."

And I knew it was God.
Not just a *don't*, but a *you're not supposed to.*

In the years leading up to that moment, I'd felt a prompting, a calling to write, to speak, to coach. But I'd dismissed it, thinking it didn't fit me. That wasn't the plan. That wasn't the ladder I had climbed.

But when everything fell away, the call remained.

So, I obeyed. Not because I wasn't afraid, but because I chose to trust.

Like Isaac, I carried the wood even when I didn't see the sacrifice. I walked forward even when the destination was unclear. I chose obedience over comfort because obedience in the face of fear builds the kind of leadership that lasts.

Biblical Reflection:

Obedience doesn't always come with clear instructions. It often asks us to take the next step without seeing the whole map. For Isaac, walking up Mount Moriah with his father was not just an act of trust in Abraham — it was trust in God's unseen plan. He didn't have all the answers, but he kept walking anyway. That's the heart of obedience: choosing to follow when clarity isn't guaranteed.

Scripture reminds us that obedience is more valuable to God than any outward show of religion or sacrifice:

> "Does the Lord delight in burnt offerings
> and sacrifices as much as in obeying the
> Lord?
> To obey is better than sacrifice, and to
> heed is better than the fat of rams."
> — 1 Samuel 15:22 (NIV)

Isaac's obedience may look quiet compared to Abraham's dramatic faith, but it was no less powerful. His willingness to trust shaped his future, his family's future, and ultimately the future of Israel. Because he obeyed, even in fear, God's covenant continued through him. Obedience doesn't just impact today — it builds legacy.

We often want obedience to feel easy or logical, but more often, it feels costly. It asks us to lay down control, our own timeline, or even our own understanding of what "should" happen. But every time we choose obedience over convenience, trust over fear, we're planting seeds that God will use to shape generations after us.

Isaac's quiet "yes" became part of a much larger story — a story that pointed forward to Jesus, the Son who also carried wood on His back up a mountain, fully obedient to His Father's will. Unlike Isaac, there was no substitute for Jesus. He became the Lamb provided for us. His obedience on the cross secured salvation for the world.

That's the power of obedience. It rarely makes sense in the moment, but it always matters. Your obedience, like Isaac's, might not look loud or dramatic, but it can echo far beyond your own life.

Obedience may feel like surrender, but in God's hands, it becomes legacy.

Leadership Lesson:

Leadership is not just about bold moves. It's about faithful ones.

Sometimes leadership looks like surrender. Sometimes it looks like saying "yes" when everything in you wants to say "not yet."

Real influence comes when you walk forward before you see the full picture.

Journal Prompts:

- When has God asked you to step into something uncomfortable?

- What fears or doubts rise up when you're called to obey?

- How could trusting God's timing strengthen your leadership?

Prayer:

Father,

You know how often fear grips my heart.
You know how I long for clarity and control.
But today, I surrender.

Help me to trust You even when the next step feels uncertain.

Help me walk with the quiet courage of Isaac —
To carry what You've given me, even when I don't yet understand why.

Let my obedience become part of Your legacy.

In Jesus' name, Amen.

Chapter 2 Wrap-Up:

Obedience often feels uncomfortable and that's okay. Real leadership isn't about always knowing the plan; it's about trusting the One who holds it.

Isaac's quiet trust on Mount Moriah shows us what it means to walk forward in faith, even when the future feels uncertain. Every act of obedience, even the trembling ones, builds a future rooted in faith.

Remember:

> It's okay to be a little uncomfortable.
> Growth and legacy live on the other side of surrender.

"Let us not become weary in doing good, for at the proper time we will reap a harvest if we do not give up."
— Galatians 6:9 (NIV)

"I'm going to have to science the heck out of this."
— Mark Watney, *The Martian*

Chapter 3: "He Kept Digging"

Dear Leader,

After stepping out in obedience, what happens when the road stretches longer than expected? What if you keep doing the right thing, but the results don't follow?

There's a special kind of tired that comes from doing the right thing over and over without seeing immediate results.

It's not dramatic.
It's not flashy.
It's the quiet kind of exhaustion that whispers, *"Is it even worth it?"*

Isaac knew that weariness.

In Genesis 26:12–22, Isaac is blessed by God and becomes wealthy. But that blessing stirs jealousy from the Philistines. Every time Isaac's servants dig a well and find water, essential for survival, the locals seize it or argue over it.

Isaac doesn't fight.
He doesn't quit.
He just moves on and digs another.

> **Genesis 26:22 (NIV):**
> *"He moved on from there and dug*

another well, and no one quarreled over it. He named it Rehoboth, saying, 'Now the Lord has given us room and we will flourish in the land.'"

Isaac models a powerful truth:

Obedience plus persistence equals legacy.
Real leaders don't let setbacks harden their hearts.
They dig again.
And again.
And again.
Until they reach the place God has prepared.

Sometimes leadership isn't about conquering battles. It's about enduring them with grace.

I can relate to Isaac's persistence in ways I never expected.

In late 2020, my husband and I launched our nonprofit. We wanted to help those in need by feeding the unhoused in our community. It wasn't a grand plan; it was a simple one. My husband would cook meals at home, and we would pack them up and go distribute them to people in need. We decided to do it once a month, just a small act of kindness in a world that often overlooks these struggles.

And yet, it hasn't been easy. Some months, it's been incredibly difficult, like fighting a losing battle. There were days I didn't want to do it, days when I felt drained and questioned if our efforts even made a difference. But we kept showing up, month after month, in faith. And in that faithfulness, God has shown us His faithfulness.

He provides what we need to cook. He provides the people who show up to help us serve. And, most importantly, He always gives us a glimpse of His love while we're serving - in a sweet smile, a hug or a testimony.

It's a beautiful thing to see how God honors our small steps of faith, even when they feel insignificant or unseen. Just like Isaac, we've kept digging. The rewards might not come immediately, but God is faithful to lead us to the places where He can use us the most.

In *The Martian*, astronaut Mark Watney finds himself stranded on Mars with limited supplies and a seemingly impossible task: survive. Faced with isolation and the harshest of conditions, he decides:

"I'm going to have to science the heck out of this."

That line stuck with me. It's not flashy or heroic. It's practical, gritty determination. It's what persistence looks like in action.

I feel like I've been in my own version of that, figuring out how to serve when we're tired, showing up without the spotlight, getting creative when resources are low.

In faith, we've had to *"dig the heck out of this."*

Just like Mark Watney used the tools he had to survive until rescue came, Isaac used the tools he had, obedience, patience, and a shovel. And in both stories, breakthrough came not by force, but through faith-filled persistence.

Biblical Reflection:

You don't have to fight every battle.
You don't have to prove yourself to every critic.
Sometimes the greatest act of leadership is quiet
endurance and peaceful movement.

Isaac's story in Genesis 26 shows us this so clearly.
Surrounded by conflict over the wells he and his
servants dug, Isaac chose not to escalate the quarrels.
Each time opposition came, he moved on and dug
again. His restraint wasn't weakness. It was wisdom.
He knew that his provision didn't ultimately come
from fighting others. It came from God.

That choice to walk away, to dig again, to trust God to
provide, is a powerful reminder that strength isn't
always about confrontation. Sometimes it's about
knowing when to stand firm and when to release
control. Isaac teaches us that peace can be more
powerful than pride.

Romans 5:3–4 (NIV) echoes this:

> "Not only so, but we also glory in our
> sufferings, because we know that suffering
> produces perseverance; perseverance,
> character; and character, hope."

Every time Isaac endured instead of fought, God was shaping his character. His perseverance wasn't passive; it was a testimony of trust. And in the end, that perseverance led to peace, the wide, open space of Rehoboth where no one fought him.

For us, this is both encouragement and challenge. Encouragement, because the opposition you face today doesn't have to define your future. Challenge, because choosing peace often takes more courage than picking a fight. But like Isaac, when you resist the urge to battle for your own name and instead trust God to provide, you make space for hope to rise.

Isaac's patience wasn't weakness. It was strength under control. It was faith in action. And it became part of his legacy.

Leadership Lesson:

When the world tries to block your wells, **keep digging**.

When others misunderstand you, **keep digging**.

When success seems slow, **keep digging**.

Persistence turns pressure into provision.

And just like Isaac, God will eventually lead you to your Rehoboth, your wide, open space.

Journal Prompts:

- What "wells" have I been digging that feel constantly contested?

- Where have I been tempted to give up lately?

- How could persistence, not pressure, be my best leadership move right now?

Prayer:

Father,

Thank You for showing me that persistence matters. Give me the strength to dig again when I feel weary.

Help me to trust that You see every effort — even the ones that go unnoticed.

Lead me to the spacious places You have prepared for me.

I choose to keep digging.

In Jesus' name, Amen.

Chapter 3 Wrap-Up:

You don't have to participate in every fight you're invited to.

Isaac's story reminds us that leadership isn't about fighting for every opportunity. It's about faithfully digging where God leads.

Persistence in the unseen places sets the foundation for a harvest you can't yet imagine.

> **Keep digging. God's promise is closer than you think.**

"I will bless you... and you will be a blessing."
— Genesis 12:2 (NIV)

"Happiness can be found even in the darkest of times, if one only remembers to turn on the light."
— Albus Dumbledore, *Harry Potter and the Prisoner of Azkaban*

Chapter 4: "Blessed to Be a Blessing"

Dear Leader,

Blessing is often misunderstood.

We tend to think of it as the reward at the end of the road, the job offer, the raise, the recognition, the answered prayer.

But in God's story, blessing is never just about what you receive.

It's about what you release.

Blessing is the beginning of something bigger than you.

> **Genesis 26:24 (NIV):**
> *"That night the Lord appeared to him and said, 'I am the God of your father Abraham. Do not be afraid, for I am with you; I will bless you and will increase the number of your descendants for the sake of my servant Abraham.'"*

God's promise to Isaac mirrored the one He gave to Abraham; a promise that carried purpose beyond personal gain.

Genesis 12:2 (NIV):

"I will bless you... and you will be a blessing."

The blessing wasn't an endpoint.
It was a launching point.
A divine invitation to become a channel, not a container.

When my husband and I started attending church regularly, we gave, like many new attendees do. We were tippers. We gave a few dollars here and there, like leaving a tip after a good meal. Grateful? Yes. Transformed? Not yet.

But over time, the Spirit nudged us toward something deeper. Something that required more than gratitude. It required trust.

We kept hearing messages about generosity. We kept encountering people who gave joyfully. And finally, we took Dave Ramsey's *Financial Peace University* class at our church. We expected to learn about budgeting. What we didn't expect was a heart shift.

We learned that giving isn't about what God needs from us. It's about what He wants for us.
Living open-handedly broke something in us, the belief that blessings were ours to hoard.

We became cheerful givers and something beautiful happened. God kept blessing us, not always in material ways, but in peace, purpose, and unexpected provision.

And every time, we remembered:

We are **blessed to be a blessing**.

Leadership can feel like a spotlight, but really, it's a lantern.

In *Harry Potter and the Prisoner of Azkaban,* Dumbledore says:

> *"Happiness can be found even in the darkest of times, if one only remembers to turn on the light."*

Leadership is like that. It's not about waiting for better conditions. It's about choosing to be the one who turns on the light. Blessing someone else with encouragement, opportunity, grace, or provision — is how we light the way through dark places.

> The biblical echo?
> God doesn't bless you just to make you comfortable.
> He blesses you to make you **a light**.

Biblical Reflection:

Blessings are not status symbols.
They are **assignments**.

Genesis 12:2 (NIV):
*"I will make you into a great nation, and
I will bless you; I will make your name
great, and you will be a blessing."*

When God blessed Isaac, it wasn't simply a private gift
for his personal comfort — it was a continuation of the
covenant He made with Abraham. In Genesis 26:24,
God appeared to Isaac and reaffirmed that promise:

Genesis 12:2 (NIV):

*"I am the God of your father Abraham. Do
not be afraid, for I am with you; I will
bless you and will increase the number of
your descendants for the sake of my
servant Abraham."*

Isaac received this word in a season when his life was
marked by movement, tension, and uncertainty. He
had just been forced to leave one place after another
because of disputes over wells. Yet instead of
retaliating or hoarding resources, Isaac kept
reopening the wells his father had dug — literal

sources of life in the desert — and giving them back to the community.

These wells were more than water; they were symbols of provision, peace, and continuity. Isaac's willingness to keep digging and keep sharing demonstrated that he understood blessing as something to be *distributed*, not just *displayed*. His enemies eventually came to him and made peace (Genesis 26:26–31), acknowledging that "We saw clearly that the LORD was with you."

Notice the divine flow:

Blessing → Greatness → Purpose → Blessing others

Isaac didn't just receive God's favor — he stewarded it so others could experience it too. His household flourished. His servants had provision. Even his rivals could not deny the reality of God's hand on him.

This is our model. God's goodness in your life is never meant to stop with you. Whether it's material provision, wisdom, influence, or opportunities, blessings are meant to travel through you to others.

When you view blessing this way, leadership shifts. It becomes less about accumulating and more about *activating*, using your influence to open wells for others, to provide space for them to flourish, and to model the kind of generosity that draws people toward God.

You're called to be a **conduit** of blessing too. God's goodness in your life was never meant to stop with you.

Leadership Lesson:

True leadership isn't about *accumulating* success. It's about *activating* it for the good of others.

You are called to make the blessings in your life **portable**, to carry light into the spaces God sends you.

Whether you lead in a boardroom, classroom, break room, or living room, your influence is a vehicle for generosity.

Leadership that gives is leadership that lasts.

Journal Prompts:

- Where have you seen God's blessings in your life recently?

- How might God be inviting you to share those blessings with others?

- What does it look like to "turn on the light" in your leadership today?

Prayer:

Father,

Thank You for every good gift You've entrusted to me.

Teach me to hold blessings with open hands, not closed fists.

Show me who I can encourage, who I can serve, and how I can be part of Your bigger story.

May my life shine Your light in every place You send me.

In Jesus' name, Amen.

Chapter 4 Wrap-Up:

Key Reminder:
You are blessed, but not just for yourself.

Your leadership is meant to create blessing **beyond you**.

Let your influence reflect God's generosity.
Let your words speak life.
Let your blessings become someone else's breakthrough.

Leadership is turning on the light, not just for yourself, but for everyone walking behind you.

"Two are better than one."
— Ecclesiastes 4:9 (NIV)

"Choosing love means choosing legacy."
— Noah, The Notebook (2004)

Chapter 5: The Right Partner Changes Everything

Dear Leader,

Isaac's marriage to Rebekah didn't just change his life, it shaped his legacy.

When Isaac's father, Abraham, knew it was time for his son to find a wife, he didn't leave it up to chance or convenience. He made sure this decision was covered in prayer and aligned with purpose. Abraham sent his servant on a mission, not just to find a woman, but to find the right partner for God's promises to continue through Isaac.

The moment Rebekah said, "I will go" (Genesis 24:58), she stepped into a story much bigger than herself. Isaac didn't chase after love out of loneliness. He waited. He trusted. And when Rebekah came, it wasn't just about romantic love, it was about a **divinely aligned partnership** in calling.

That's what true partnership is, it multiplies purpose.

I didn't always understand that.

Growing up, I didn't imagine myself ever getting married. Raised by a strong, independent single mom, in a neighborhood full of women who carried everything on their own, I planned to follow the same path. I figured I'd be a single mom too, and I was perfectly fine with that. I didn't think I needed anyone.

But God had other plans.

This year, my husband and I are celebrating 25 years of marriage and we're still going strong. It wasn't always easy, especially for someone as fiercely independent as I was. But with God's grace and my husband's incredible patience, I learned a truth that changed not just my life but the legacy we're building: **two really are better than one.**

Our marriage didn't just change me, it changed the story we're writing for our children. We are a team, and I wouldn't have it any other way.

It reminds me of a line from *The Notebook*, where Noah says,

"Choosing love means choosing legacy."

Our relationships **do** shape our legacy in our homes, our leadership, and our faith walk.

> Maybe you've been burned before.
> Maybe trusting someone felt like weakness, or you were taught that needing others made you less of a leader.
> But that's not God's design. Jesus chose

twelve. Paul had Barnabas. Isaac had Rebekah.

You're not meant to do this alone, not because you can't, but because you weren't created to.

In your leadership journey, the people you choose to walk with will shape the influence you carry. Whether it's a spouse, a friend, a colleague, or a mentor, those relationships matter deeply. They will either strengthen your calling or distract you from it.

Choose wisely. Choose prayerfully. Choose with legacy in mind.

Biblical Reflection:

Isaac's partnership with Rebekah wasn't just personal; it was purposeful. Scripture tells us she became a comfort to him after his mother's death (Genesis 24:67). That detail may seem small, but it highlights the relational side of God's blessings. Rebekah wasn't simply an answer to Isaac's need for a wife, she was an answer to his need for companionship, encouragement, and partnership in God's greater plan.

When Abraham's servant arrived at Rebekah's household, the decision to leave everything behind and join Isaac's journey wasn't easy. But when her family asked if she was willing, she responded with bold simplicity: *"I will go"* (Genesis 24:58). That yes, that courageous step of obedience, positioned her not only as Isaac's partner, but as a key player in the unfolding of God's promise to Abraham. Through Isaac and Rebekah, the family line of Israel would continue.

Her yes reminds us that legacy often hinges on everyday choices. Sometimes the greatest acts of faith don't come with fanfare but with willingness: to leave what's familiar, to trust God's leading, and to step into an uncertain future with courage.

Ecclesiastes 4:9–12 (NIV) reminds us why partnership matters:

> "Two are better than one, because they
> have a good return for their labor:
> If either of them falls down, one can help
> the other up.
> But pity anyone who falls and has no one
> to help them up.
> Also, if two lie down together, they will
> keep warm.
> But how can one keep warm alone?
> Though one may be overpowered, two can
> defend themselves.
> A cord of three strands is not quickly
> broken."

This passage doesn't just apply to marriage. It applies to leadership, community, and the relationships God calls us to steward. Isaac and Rebekah's partnership illustrates this truth. Their combined faith, their shared journey, and their alignment with God's promise created a foundation that was stronger than either could have built alone.

In leadership, this reminds us that we aren't meant to carry the weight of our calling alone. God often sends people, mentors, friends, colleagues, or spouses, to walk alongside us. The question is: will we say yes to those partnerships, and will we nurture them in ways that honor God's bigger story?

Isaac and Rebekah's union shows us that when God brings people together for His purposes, the result is more than comfort — it's legacy.

Leadership Lesson:

Leadership isn't a solo act. It's a team effort.

The partnerships you nurture, whether in marriage, mentorship, ministry, or friendship, directly impact your legacy. When you walk with people who align with your values and vision, your influence grows beyond what you could build alone.

Isaac's story reminds us: When we trust God with our relationships, **He multiplies our impact.**

Journal Prompts:

- Who in your life consistently strengthens your faith and leadership?

- Are there relationships God might be calling you to invest in more deeply, or even to step away from?

- How can you become the kind of partner, friend, or teammate who builds others up for God's purposes?

Prayer:

Father,

Thank You for the people You have placed in my life. Help me to choose relationships wisely — partnerships that point me back to You.

Teach me to be a faithful friend, a steady encourager, and a trustworthy leader.

Remind me that I do not walk this journey alone, and that Your Spirit leads me in every connection You ordain.

In Jesus' name, Amen.

Chapter 5 Wrap-Up:

Isaac's marriage to Rebekah was more than a love story. It was a partnership that shaped their leadership and legacy.

And the same is true for us.

You don't have to walk this leadership journey alone.

Trust God with the people He places in your life and be intentional about the relationships you build.

Surround yourself with those who strengthen your purpose, and you'll find that your influence will grow beyond what you could do on your own.

The right partner, whether in marriage, friendship, or work, has the power to change everything.

Choose with trust. Walk with purpose. Watch your legacy unfold.

"Let perseverance finish its work so that you may be mature and complete, not lacking anything."
— James 1:4 (NIV)

"Wax on, wax off."
— *Mr. Miyagi, The Karate Kid*
(1984)

Chapter 6: Patient with the Process

Dear Leader,

Patience is a virtue... right? That's what they say. But let's be honest, whoever "they" are clearly haven't sat in traffic, waited on a delayed flight, or tried to sit still while their plans crumbled in front of them.

I used to think patience meant doing nothing, just twiddling my thumbs while life stalled. But I've come to learn that real patience is anything but passive. It's one of the hardest, holiest forms of discipline there is.

And full confession: I've struggled with it.

I'm a planner. A spreadsheet-for-everything, calendar-color-coded, what's-next-and-how-do-we-get-there kind of planner. I like movement. I like progress. I like knowing exactly how things will unfold.

So when God disrupts my timeline, my inner GPS starts yelling, "Recalculating!"

But over the years, in His relentless love and grace, God has kept inviting me into seasons where I had no choice but to wait. And I'm finally learning that these pauses are not punishment. They are preparation.

As *Proverbs 19:21* reminds us:

"Many are the plans in a person's heart,
but it is the Lord's purpose that prevails."

Isaac understood this.

We often talk about Isaac as the "bridge" between
Abraham and Jacob, the quiet one, the obedient son,
the faithful husband. But let's zoom in on one part of
his story that often gets overlooked: *the wait*.

Isaac was 40 when he married Rebekah. He was 60
when their sons, Jacob and Esau, were born. **Twenty
years.**

That's not a short delay. That's two decades of
watching and wondering. Two decades of "Lord,
when?" Two decades of growing older, while nothing
seemed to change.

And yet we don't read anywhere in the Bible that Isaac
abandoned the promise. He didn't grow bitter. He
didn't find a backup plan like his mother Sarah did
with Hagar.

Instead, he *prayed*.

> *"Isaac prayed to the Lord on behalf of his
> wife, because she was childless. The Lord
> answered his prayer, and his wife*

Rebekah became pregnant."
    — Genesis 25:21 (NIV)

This wasn't resignation. It was resilience. Isaac chose *prayer over panic*. He trusted God not only with the *what*, but with the *when*. That's leadership. That's legacy.

In *The Karate Kid*, Daniel is frustrated. He wants to learn karate — *not now but right now*. Instead, Mr. Miyagi hands him a sponge and a bucket.

"Wax on. Wax off."

Daniel doesn't realize that the monotonous chores, washing cars, sanding floors, painting fences, are building muscle memory, strength, and discipline. He feels stuck. But he's being shaped.

When the real fight comes, everything clicks into place. What felt like wasted time was actually a training *ground*.

Leadership is the same.

God's "wax on, wax off" moments are all around us: when we're asked to serve behind the scenes, when a promotion stalls, when a dream stays dormant. We think we're standing still. But He's strengthening us for the next stage.

Biblical Reflection:

Isaac's twenty-year wait wasn't dead space. It was divine development. What felt like delay was really God's design. The years between promise and fulfillment were not wasted; they were sacred. God used them to refine Isaac's patience, stretch his faith, and shape him into the kind of leader who could father not just two sons, but nations.

It would have been easy for Isaac and Rebekah to grow bitter or hopeless in the waiting. But instead, Isaac prayed (Genesis 25:21). That single verse speaks volumes. In seasons when he had no control over the outcome, Isaac chose to place what he *couldn't* do in the hands of the One who could. And God answered.

This shows us something important: waiting isn't punishment — it's preparation. God often allows waiting seasons because He knows what's coming next will require deeper roots, stronger faith, and fuller trust than we have right now. Isaac's twenty-year delay meant that by the time Jacob and Esau arrived, their father had been formed into a man who understood perseverance.

James 1:4 (NIV) says it plainly:

"Let perseverance finish its work so that you may be mature and complete, not lacking anything."

That's exactly what God was doing in Isaac. The waiting wasn't failure. It was formation. It was God's way of maturing him for the blessing that was still on the way.

And isn't that the story of so much of Scripture? Abraham and Sarah waiting decades for Isaac. Joseph waiting years in slavery and prison before leading Egypt. David waiting to take the throne after being anointed king. Even the disciples waited in Jerusalem for the coming of the Holy Spirit. Waiting is not a detour in God's plan — it's often the very path that prepares us for it.

So when you find yourself in a season of waiting — whether for an opportunity, a breakthrough, or an answered prayer — remember Isaac. God was working in the silence, shaping something in him that would sustain the weight of the promise. And He's doing the same in you.

Waiting doesn't mean you're forgotten. It means God is growing you into someone who can carry the blessing when it comes.

Leadership Lesson:

Leadership is rarely a sprint. It's a slow, steady climb that requires:

- Vision without full visibility

- Hope without immediate evidence

- Faith without fast-forward

True leaders don't just survive the wait. They *grow* in it. They let perseverance do its work. They wax on. Wax off.

Journal Prompts:

- Where in your leadership journey are you currently waiting?

- What "wax on, wax off" routines might God be using to prepare you?

- In what areas are you being invited to release control and lean into trust?

Prayer:

Lord,

Teach me to wait with purpose.
Help me resist the urge to rush ahead of You.
Remind me that Your delays are never denials —
they're divine shaping.
Make me faithful in the small things.
Patient in the slow things.
And hopeful in all things.

Even when I don't see movement, I know You are
working.

Build in me the strength to endure and the faith to
keep showing up.

In Jesus' name, Amen.

Chapter 6 Wrap-Up:

Isaac waited two decades for a promise to bloom, and when it did, the fruit changed history. He didn't force the outcome. He didn't quit halfway through. He stayed in the process.

So can you.

Leadership isn't about everything going according to plan. It's about letting God rework the plan and shape the leader in ways we never expected.

So if you're stuck in a season of spiritual chores or stalled timelines, remember:

Wax on. Wax off.

You're not wasting time.
 You're training for what's next.

Let patience finish its work so you may be mature, complete, and ready when the promise comes.

"Train up a child in the way he should go, and when he is old, he will not depart from it."
— Proverbs 22:6 (NIV)

"Everyone in the family has a different gift."
— *Encanto* (2021)

Chapter 7: "When Your Kids Don't Get It"

Dear Leader,

Parenting and leadership often walk the same tightrope, loving deeply while letting go. You guide, nurture, and pour your heart into those you lead, hoping they'll understand the weight of your investment. But what happens when they just don't get it? When their choices break your heart or go in a direction you never imagined?

I remember one of the hardest seasons in our home. Our daughter was making a decision about her life that I didn't agree with, one I thought would derail her future. I believed I was protecting her, but in truth, I was trying to control her. What I thought was love came out as fear, and that fear showed up as anger, arguments, and a grip I refused to loosen. The atmosphere in our home turned ugly, and I was a huge contributor to that ugliness.

It wasn't until later, much later, that I realized I needed to step out of the way and let God do the watering. I had planted seeds all throughout her childhood, but I was trying to force them to grow on my schedule. I often say, *"Parents do the best they can in the time they're in with the information they have."* A sister in Christ once told me, "I don't like that phrase. It feels like a cop-out." But I don't believe it is. I believe it's grace. Parenting isn't about perfection. It's about showing up, learning, and trusting God with the rest.

Isaac knew that tension well. He had two sons, Esau and Jacob, who couldn't have been more different. Esau, rugged and favored by Isaac, seemed to be the son who would carry on the legacy. Jacob, more reserved and favored by Rebekah, Isaac's wife, would ultimately receive the blessing that shaped generations. Isaac didn't see it coming. When the deception unfolded and he realized he had been tricked, the Bible says he "trembled violently" (Genesis 27:33 NIV). But even in that trembling, Isaac didn't reverse course. He accepted what had happened and affirmed the blessing: *"Indeed he will be blessed"* (Genesis 27:33 NIV).

That moment, as painful and confusing as it must have been, showed a shift in Isaac. He let go of his own expectations and trusted that God's plan was still moving forward, even if it looked nothing like what he envisioned. That's leadership. That's parenting. Not perfect control, but faithful surrender.

In *Encanto*, we watch a family where every member has a unique gift, but they struggle to see the value in each other's strengths. Misunderstandings and unmet expectations create fractures, but healing comes when they learn to see and honor each other's journeys.

That's what Isaac had to do. And that's what I had to do, too. I had to stop seeing my daughter's choices as personal failures and start trusting that the God who created her would be faithful to finish the work He started in her.

Whether you're parenting, leading a team, or mentoring others, sometimes the people closest to you won't "get it," not right away. But you can trust that the seeds you've sown are not wasted. God is faithful to bring growth in His time.

Biblical Reflection:

Isaac's journey with Esau and Jacob is a powerful reminder that leadership, especially within families, doesn't come with guarantees. You can model wisdom, you can teach faithfully, you can pray fervently, but at the end of the day, each person must choose their own path.

Esau chose the temporary over the eternal. Selling his birthright for a single meal (Genesis 25:29–34) revealed how little he valued the inheritance and covenant God had entrusted to their family. Isaac had every reason to be disappointed, maybe even angry. Then later, when Jacob deceived both his brother and his father to receive the blessing, Isaac could have reacted with rage, withdrawn his blessing, or cursed Jacob's actions. Instead, Scripture records something remarkable: "Isaac trembled violently... and he said, 'Indeed, he will be blessed'" (Genesis 27:33, NIV).

That moment wasn't resignation. It was surrender. Isaac understood that God's plan was bigger than his own expectations, and even in the pain of deception, he trusted that God's purposes would prevail. It takes deep humility to accept outcomes you didn't plan for and still say, "God's will be done."

As leaders, this is one of the hardest lessons we learn. We plant seeds of truth, integrity, and faith and then we want to control how, when, and if they grow. But leadership, like parenting, requires surrender. We must release the outcome and trust that God waters what we cannot.

Proverbs 22:6 reminds us: *"Train up a child in the way he should go, and when he is old, he will not depart from it."* This verse isn't a formula with guaranteed timing. It's a promise that seeds planted in love and truth will not be wasted. Even when there are detours, rebellion, or seasons of wandering, God honors the investment of faithful leadership.

Isaac's story shows us that surrender is not weakness. It is faith. He let go of control and allowed God to direct the legacy. And that is often the hardest, but most powerful, act of leadership we can offer.

———————————————————————————

Leadership Lesson:

As a leader, you are called to guide, not to control. And when the people you lead choose differently than you hoped, it doesn't mean your leadership was wasted.

Isaac shows us that leadership includes letting go. He didn't try to reverse the blessing. He didn't lash out. He trembled, then surrendered. That's grace under pressure.

Whether you're leading a child, mentoring a colleague, or shepherding a group, there will be moments when it feels like all your investment has gone unnoticed. But God sees. He's still at work. Leadership isn't about micromanaging the outcome; it's about being faithful to the process and trusting God with the harvest.

Journal Prompts:

- What areas of your leadership have you tried to control that you need to surrender to God?

- When has God asked you to trust Him, even when your leadership didn't seem to be making an impact?

- How can you lead with love and wisdom, even when those you lead don't fully understand or follow your guidance?

Prayer:

Father,

Thank You for the trust You place in me to lead those around me.

Help me to remember that I cannot control the choices of others, but I can trust You with the results.

Teach me to lead with wisdom, patience, and love, even when it feels like those I lead don't understand or appreciate it.

Give me the strength to walk in faith, trusting that You are at work in the hearts of those I lead.

In Jesus' name, Amen.

Chapter 7 Wrap-Up:

Isaac's leadership teaches us that we can't control the actions of others, but we can be faithful in our example. Whether you're leading a team, your family, or your community, remember that you are planting seeds of influence. Trust that God will use those seeds in His timing. Your role is to lead with love, to model integrity, and to surrender the rest to the One who sees the whole story.

"Be still and know that I am God."
— Psalm 46:10 (NIV)

"Silence doesn't mean the absence of strength."
— *A Quiet Place* (2018)

Chapter 8:
Blessing in the Quiet

Dear Leader,

Introvert here. Quiet is my favorite. My sweet spot. I love spending quiet time with God. When the noise fades, the meetings, the opinions, the pressure to perform, I finally feel like I can breathe. That's when I hear Him most clearly.

For a long time, I thought leadership had to be loud. That it meant standing at the front of the room, commanding attention, always having something to say. But over the years, I've learned that some of the strongest leaders lead in stillness. And that kind of leadership isn't weak, it's sacred.

Isaac's life reminds us of this truth. His leadership wasn't loud or dramatic, but his quiet influence helped shape the future of Israel.

Genesis 27:28–29 (NIV) says:

> *"May God give you heaven's dew and earth's richness — an abundance of grain and new wine. May nations serve you and peoples bow down to you. Be lord over your brothers, and may the sons of your mother bow down to you. May those who curse you be cursed and those who bless you be blessed."*

Isaac's blessing over Jacob wasn't just a transfer of material wealth. It was a spiritual handoff, a declaration of identity and divine purpose. And it happened quietly. No audience. No fanfare. Just a father, a son, and the weight of God's promise. That quiet moment set the course for generations.

Isaac's story isn't filled with dramatic scenes or heroic battles. His is a story of steady faith, of digging wells, waiting patiently, trusting God through uncertainty. His silence wasn't passive; it was purposeful. He knew how to be still and let God lead. That takes more strength than most people realize.

Think about *A Quiet Place*. The family didn't survive by making noise. They survived by staying quiet, being intentional, and moving in unity. Their strength was found in discipline, not in volume. That's what quiet leadership looks like. It's not about how loudly you lead, but how faithfully you follow.

There is power in restraint. In waiting. In praying quietly when the world is shouting.

There's blessing in the quiet.

Biblical Reflection:

Isaac didn't need a stage to be impactful. His quiet leadership was grounded in deep faith and unwavering trust in God. His influence didn't come from armies, speeches, or dramatic gestures. It came from stillness; the kind that listens, trusts, and waits for God to move.

Psalm 46:10 reminds us:
"Be still, and know that I am God."

The world tells us to hustle harder, speak louder, prove more. But Scripture calls us to a different rhythm, one of sacred quiet. Stillness isn't passivity. It's not disengagement or apathy. It is strength wrapped in surrender, an act of trust that says, "God, You are enough. You are in control, even if I'm not."

Isaac lived this out. He wasn't chasing visibility. He wasn't desperate to be heard. He simply walked in obedience and did what God asked of him. And because of that, he became a key part of God's redemptive plan. His role may not have been as dramatic as Abraham's or Jacob's, but without Isaac's quiet faithfulness, the story of Israel would have no bridge between promise and fulfillment.

Stillness is not inactivity. It is intentional trust. It is choosing not to strive, not to manipulate outcomes, and not to let fear dictate your next step. It is the discipline of stepping back so God can step in.

In leadership, stillness might not look productive, but it is powerful. Quiet leaders, like Isaac, remind us that the deepest impact often comes not through noise but through peace. When you lead from stillness, praying, waiting, trusting, you make room for God to move in ways you could never orchestrate on your own.

Leadership Lesson:

Leadership doesn't require a stage or spotlight. Some of the most effective leadership happens behind the scenes, in prayer, preparation, and patience.

Isaac's influence came through quiet obedience. He trusted God even when the path was unclear. He made choices rooted in faith, not ambition. And his legacy still echoes because of it.

As a leader, you don't have to be the loudest voice in the room. In fact, there's strength in stepping back and choosing stillness.

Like the family in *A Quiet Place*, sometimes the greatest impact comes from quiet discipline, intentional action, and unwavering trust.

Let go of the pressure to perform. Let go of the fear that quiet equals insignificance.
 God may be doing His greatest work in you, and through you, in the quiet.

Journal Prompts:

- In what areas of your leadership can you embrace quiet moments of reflection and stillness?

- How can you be more intentional about leading without needing the spotlight?

- What would it look like for you to trust God's timing in your leadership without rushing to make things happen?

Prayer:

Father,

Thank You for the quiet moments that help me hear Your voice more clearly.

Remind me that leadership doesn't have to be loud, sometimes it's about being faithful in the stillness.

Give me the strength to trust You in the quiet.

Shape me into a leader who walks in step with Your timing, not mine.

May I lead with humility, integrity, and peace.

In Jesus' name, Amen.

Chapter 8 Wrap-Up:

Isaac's life shows us that quiet leadership is powerful.
He didn't need noise or attention to be effective.
He trusted God in stillness, and that stillness laid the
foundation for generations to come.

Don't be afraid of the quiet.
That may be the very space where your greatest
influence begins.

Let God meet you there.
Let Him lead.

And trust that even in the silence, especially in the
silence, He's doing something big.

"Whatever you do, work at it with all your heart, as working for the Lord, not for human masters."
— *Colossians 3:23 (NIV)*

"Sometimes I'll start a sentence, and I don't even know where it's going. I just hope I find it along the way."
— Michael Scott, The Office

Chapter 9:
"Faith in the Mundane"

Dear Leader,

In a world that celebrates "overnight success" and chases the next big moment, the slow and steady rhythm of ordinary days can feel... well, disappointing. We scroll through filtered highlight reels and forget that real leadership, the kind that transforms, is rarely exciting, and almost never instant.

Sometimes, the bravest thing you can do as a leader is just keep showing up.

I've sat across from team members frustrated not because they were doing poorly, but because they weren't doing "great," at least not in the social media sense of the word. No one was filming them answering emails. There was no applause for filing reports or staying calm in meetings. The work felt small, so they felt small. And that's the danger, when we start measuring the value of our contribution by the amount of attention it gets.

But faithfulness doesn't need a spotlight.

Just ask Isaac.

Isaac's leadership moment wasn't in a great speech, a daring rescue, or a dramatic battle. It was in reopening wells, literal, dusty, clogged-up wells that his father Abraham had dug. The Philistines had filled them with dirt after Abraham's death, so Isaac returned to clear them out. Not glamorous. Not viral. Just faithful.

> "Isaac reopened the wells that had been dug in the time of his father Abraham, which the Philistines had stopped up after Abraham died, and he gave them the same names his father had given them."
> — *Genesis 26:18 (NIV)*

What a picture of leadership, honoring legacy, restoring provision, reclaiming purpose. It was slow work. Dirty work. But it was meaningful.

And maybe that's where we get it twisted. We confuse *flashy* with *fruitful*.

Isaac's obedience in the mundane made room for blessing. And your obedience in the emails, the spreadsheets, the carpool lines, the staff meetings is making room too. It's digging space for something deeper: trust, character, impact.

I laugh every time I hear Michael Scott say, *"Sometimes I'll start a sentence, and I don't even know where it's going."* It's funny because it's true, especially for leaders. There are days we're just figuring it out as we go, wondering if any of this matters, hoping we land somewhere good. But here's what anchors us: our "why."

> "Whatever you do, work at it with all your heart, as working for the Lord, not for human masters,"
> — *Colossians 3:23 (NIV)*

When your work is for the Lord, the "what" doesn't have to be flashy. It just has to be faithful.

So, leader, if your current season feels repetitive, unnoticed, or dry, keep digging. Keep showing up. God is present in the monotony. He is working in the unseen. And those daily acts of diligence? They're building wells of blessing for those who will come after you.

Biblical Reflection:

Isaac's story is a reminder that sacred work often looks ordinary. His legacy wasn't built on loud victories or dramatic acts of heroism. It was built on the quiet work of faithfulness. He didn't rush to reinvent. He reopened the wells his father Abraham had dug. He reclaimed what was lost. He served without spotlight.

That's not weakness. That's spiritual maturity. It takes strength to remain steady when the world demands constant innovation, applause, or recognition. Isaac shows us that ordinary faithfulness is extraordinary in God's eyes.

Colossians 3:23 (NIV) reminds us:
"Whatever you do, work at it with all your heart, as working for the Lord, not for human masters."

Notice the word *whatever*. Not just the big projects. Not just the public roles. Whatever. That includes the small tasks no one else notices, the meeting prep, the spreadsheets, the bedtime routines and the daily conversations.

What if you approached your routine tasks as holy ground? That commute. That phone call. That meal you prepare. That small act of kindness. All of it becomes sacred when done in His name.

Jesus Himself modeled this truth. Before His public ministry, He spent years as a carpenter, faithful in the mundane, working with His hands, honoring the Father in ordinary labor. And when His ministry began, He often pointed to the everyday, seeds in soil, lamps on stands, birds in the air, as the backdrop for eternal truth.

Isaac's wells may have seemed ordinary, but they sustained life for his people and carried forward the blessing of Abraham. Your faithfulness in the "mundane" carries the same potential, to water others, to restore what was lost, and to create space for God's promise to flourish.

Leadership Lesson:

Real leadership is found in the consistency of your character, not the attention you receive. Isaac shows us that impact isn't always loud, but it's always rooted in faithfulness.

Your quiet consistency is creating a legacy. The world may never applaud the well you dug, but God will use it to bless generations.

Journal Prompts:

- Where in your life have you undervalued the importance of the "small" or unseen work?

- How can you shift your mindset to see everyday tasks as worship?

- What well are you being called to reopen, something old, faithful, forgotten, that still holds purpose?

Prayer:

Father,

Thank You for reminding me that You meet me in the mundane. When I feel unseen or unimportant, help me remember that You see me. Help me to work with excellence in the small things, knowing that nothing is wasted in Your kingdom. May my heart find joy in the routines, the repetition, and the restoration. Use my ordinary days for extraordinary impact.

In Jesus' name, Amen.

Chapter 9 Wrap-Up:

Isaac led by quietly restoring what had been lost. He honored the past and made room for the future, not with noise, but with steady obedience.

So, the next time your work feels "just average," remember this: God is in the average. And through your faithfulness, He's doing something eternal.

Keep digging.

"Well done, good and faithful servant."
— Matthew 25:23 (NIV)

"Remember no man is a failure who has friends."
— Clarence, *It's a Wonderful Life*

Chapter 10: Legacy Isn't Loud

Dear Leader,

There's something powerful about quiet faithfulness. It doesn't demand attention or chase applause, but it leaves a mark that lasts far beyond the moment. Isaac's life was like that, a legacy formed not by loud declarations or dramatic victories, but by steady obedience and peaceful leadership.

I often think about the legacy I left during my years in corporate America. Titles came and went, projects launched and closed, but what stayed with me, and what I hope stayed with the people I led, was a deep sense of care. My main job wasn't just to hit goals or produce numbers. It was to make sure people were taken care of.

I truly believed, and still believe, that when people are supported physically, emotionally, and spiritually, they can work in peace. And when people work in peace, they thrive. Teams flourish. Results come naturally. My joy came from helping others grow and succeed, knowing that when they did, the whole team rose together. And as a result, the impact to the company's success was both measurable and meaningful, built not just on performance, but on people who felt valued and empowered to do their best work.

A lot of companies say, "We're like a family," often as a way to get more from people without giving more to them. But for me, it was never about a slogan. I meant it. I wanted people to know they mattered, not just for what they could do, but for who they were. Many of my old coworkers are still close friends today, and I believe that's because I cultivated a culture of genuine care.

That's the kind of legacy Isaac left. In *Genesis 26:24*, God appears to Isaac and says,

"I am the God of your father Abraham. Do not be afraid, for I am with you."

That wasn't just reassurance for a hard moment. It was a generational promise. Isaac's quiet faithfulness was the bridge between the call of Abraham and the future of Israel.

Like Isaac, you may not always see the fruit of your faithfulness right away. But leadership that is rooted in care, integrity, and trust has a ripple effect. That's what Clarence reminded George Bailey of in *It's a Wonderful Life*.

"Remember, no man is a failure who has friends."

George didn't see the impact of his life until someone helped him step back. And sometimes we need that reminder too, that what we're building in the quiet matters more than we know.

So keep leading in love. Keep showing up with compassion. The impact of your faithful leadership may not be loud, but it will last.

Biblical Reflection:

Isaac didn't have a dramatic ministry or lead armies into battle. He didn't chase platforms or power. But his life was deeply significant in the story of God's people. He trusted God. He moved when God said move. He stayed when God said stay. And he lived a life that honored God in everyday obedience.

Matthew 25:23 reminds us that God sees the quiet things:
"His master replied, 'Well done, good and faithful servant! You have been faithful with a few things; I will put you in charge of many things. Come and share your master's happiness!'"

That verse isn't just for the celebrated or spotlighted. It's for the ones who choose faithfulness when no one else sees. Isaac's story is proof that God builds legacies on trust and obedience more than performance or fame.

What's even more powerful is that Jesus Himself confirms Isaac's place in God's eternal story. In Matthew 22:32, Jesus identifies the Lord as *"the God of Abraham, the God of Isaac, and the God of Jacob."* Think about that for a moment. Isaac's name is forever spoken by the Son of God as part of the covenant lineage. His quiet obedience placed him in the center of God's unfolding redemption plan.

Isaac reminds us that legacy is not about being remembered by crowds but about being remembered by God. His story calls us to reframe our own definition of success. Faithful obedience in the ordinary moments matters more than public victories. Quiet trust matters more than loud recognition.

And here's the good news: the same God who wove Isaac's name into His covenant story is writing your story too. If you remain faithful, your obedience, no matter how small or hidden, becomes part of a legacy that outlives you.

Leadership Lesson:

Legacy isn't measured in applause. It's measured in impact.

The best leaders don't just lead well in public, they care deeply in private. They make sure their people are seen, heard, and supported. They build trust, not for recognition, but because it's the right thing to do.

Isaac didn't make noise. He made history. His steady, faithful leadership positioned the next generation to thrive. And that's the kind of leader we're all invited to be.

Faithful. Consistent. Quiet, but deeply impactful.

Journal Prompts:

- What are some small, quiet acts of faith you've made that you believe God is using?

- How can you build a lasting legacy through your everyday choices?

- What kind of legacy do you want to leave for future generations?

Prayer:

Father,

Thank You for reminding me that faithfulness in the quiet moments matters.

Help me to live each day with the kind of integrity and devotion that builds a legacy for Your Kingdom.

May I trust that You are at work in the small, faithful steps I take, and may my life be a reflection of Your goodness for generations to come.

In Jesus' name, Amen.

Chapter 10 Wrap-Up:

Isaac's story teaches us that legacy isn't built through noise. It's built through faithfulness. You don't need to be the loudest or the most visible to make a difference. What matters most is how you show up for others, how you walk with God, and how you live with intention and care.

Quiet leaders change the world, not all at once, but step by faithful step.

Conclusion: You Don't Have to Be Loud to Be Legendary

Isaac's life reminds us that leadership doesn't always roar.

Sometimes it whispers. Sometimes it is steady, consistent, or grounded in quiet obedience.

Sometimes it moves like a slow, faithful river, carving legacy not through grand gestures, but through daily choices that honor God.

He wasn't the loudest patriarch.
He wasn't known for battles or speeches.
But he trusted.
He waited.
He persevered.
He blessed the next generation.

His legacy wasn't defined by titles or applause. It was defined by trust. By obedience. By peace.

And maybe, just maybe, that's the kind of leader you're being called to be, too.

You don't have to shout to be heard.

You don't have to strive for the spotlight to make a difference.

You don't have to chase influence to leave impact.

Your quiet faithfulness, the unseen decisions, the hard moments when you chose integrity, the gentle ways you showed up for others, those are the seeds of something eternal.

You are leading.
With care. With purpose. With quiet strength.
And that matters more than you know.

Even Jesus pointed to Isaac when affirming the promises of God. In Matthew 8:11 (NIV), He says,

> *"I say to you that many will come from the east and the west and will take their places at the feast with Abraham, **Isaac**, and Jacob in the kingdom of heaven."*

Isaac is there, named by Jesus Himself. Not forgotten. Not overlooked. Seated at the table of legacy in God's Kingdom. That is the reward of quiet faithfulness: eternity written with your name on it.

So lead boldly in your own way.
Not for applause. Not for performance. But for purpose.

Because in God's Kingdom, faithfulness always leaves a mark.

And in the end, the quiet ones, the ones who served, waited, loved, and trusted, often leave the loudest legacy.

Well done, good and faithful servant.

Now go lead, just as He made you to.

Bonus Content

Hey friend,

Before you close this book, I want to leave you with a little more encouragement.

Leadership isn't one-size-fits-all. Some leaders are loud and energetic. Others are quiet and steady. Both can change the world.

In the next few pages, you'll find a few bonus sections, a little extra to remind you that however you lead, your voice matters.

Take your time with them. Reflect. And remember: Quiet leadership is still powerful leadership.

Bonus Content A: Quiet Leaders vs. Loud Leaders in the Bible

Quote:
"The best leaders are those the people hardly know exist." — Lao Tzu

Content:
In Scripture, leadership shows up in very different ways:

- **Moses** was bold and visible — parting seas, confronting kings, leading masses.

- **David** was passionate — defeating giants, leading armies, writing psalms.

- **Paul** was a tireless speaker — traveling, preaching, planting churches.

Isaac, however, led quietly — living faithfully, digging wells, shepherding a family.
The contrast is important:
Loud isn't better. Quiet isn't lesser.
Both are essential in God's story.

Isaac's leadership style reminds us:

- Trust can be louder than speeches.

- Consistency can be more lasting than grand gestures.

- Faithfulness in the unseen matters deeply.

Reflection Question:
Are you trying to lead like someone you weren't called to be?

Bonus Content B: Quiet Leaders in History and Today

Quote:
"Not all of us can do great things. But we can do small things with great love." — Mother Teresa

Content:
World-changers often lead without making noise:

- **Fred Rogers** gently taught kindness and emotional intelligence through everyday TV episodes.

- **Mother Teresa** served millions without seeking headlines, loving the "least of these" in Calcutta.

- **Jane Goodall** quietly and patiently revolutionized conservation work.

- **Mister Miyagi** (fictional, *The Karate Kid*) trained a champion with humble tasks rather than dramatic speeches.

Each of them led by **faithfulness, gentleness, and steadfastness**, much like Isaac.

Quiet leadership leaves deep, wide ripples — often unseen until long after the work is done.

Reflection Question:
Who are the quiet leaders that have impacted your life?

Bonus Content C: Leadership Styles Quiz: Are You a Quiet or Bold Leader?

Quote:
"There are different kinds of service, but the same Lord." — 1 Corinthians 12:5

Quiz:

1. When faced with a challenge, you usually:
   a) Rally a team and tackle it loudly.
   b) Step back, observe, and plan a quiet solution.

2. In a group, people would describe you as:
   a) Energetic and inspiring.
   b) Wise and steady.

3. You prefer to influence others by:
   a) Publicly inspiring them with big ideas.
   b) Privately mentoring and modeling

consistency.

4. You feel energized when:
   a) Launching new, exciting initiatives.
   b) Building a strong, lasting foundation behind the scenes.

Mostly A's:
You lean toward **Bold Leadership** — energetic, visible, inspiring change through action and words.

Mostly B's:
You lean toward **Quiet Leadership** — steady, faithful, influencing through actions and presence.

Final Thought:
Whether loud or quiet, both styles reflect the heart of leadership when surrendered to God.

Reflection Challenge:
Ask yourself:
"How can I better embrace the leadership style God gave me?"

Bibliography

The Holy Bible, New International Version (NIV). Biblica, 2011.

Walt Disney Animation Studios. *Moana*. Directed by Ron Clements and John Musker. Walt Disney Studios Motion Pictures, 2016.

Marvel Entertainment. *Spider-Man*. Directed by Sam Raimi. Columbia Pictures, 2002.

20th Century Fox. *The Martian*. Directed by Ridley Scott. 20th Century Fox, 2015.

Marvel Studios. *Black Panther*. Directed by Ryan Coogler. Walt Disney Studios Motion Pictures, 2018.

New Line Cinema. *The Notebook*. Directed by Nick Cassavetes. New Line Cinema, 2004.

Columbia Pictures. *The Karate Kid*. Directed by John G. Avildsen. Columbia Pictures, 1984.

Walt Disney Animation Studios. *Encanto*. Directed by Jared Bush and Byron Howard. Walt Disney Studios Motion Pictures, 2021.

Paramount Pictures. *A Quiet Place*. Directed by John Krasinski. Paramount Pictures, 2018.

NBC. *The Office*. Created by Greg Daniels. NBC, 2005–2013.

Liberty Films. *It's a Wonderful Life*. Directed by Frank Capra. RKO Radio Pictures, 1946.

Muñiz, Myriam. *Momentum Moves Mountains*. Personal leadership reflections, 2025.

Unvarsky, Sue. Personal mentorship quote, 2025.

Acknowledgments

Writing *Isaac: A Model of Quiet Leadership* has been a journey of reflection, faith, and gratitude. I am deeply thankful for the people who encouraged me along the way.

To my mentors, **Sue Unvarsky** and **Olivia Eaddy** — your wisdom, encouragement, and timely words of truth have shaped not only this book but my life. Thank you for reminding me that it's okay to be a little uncomfortable and that faithful conversations can change the course of a day, or a life.

To my dear friends **Kristin Dishaw** and **Sherita Jackson** — thank you for continuing to walk beside me, reading drafts, and giving the most honest, thoughtful feedback. Your support makes me braver, and your belief in me keeps this dream alive.

To my daughter **Zahra**, my favorite editor and creative partner — I'm making you work hard, but you keep showing up with sharp eyes and a soft heart. Thank you for being the quiet strength behind the scenes, just like Isaac.

To my **husband** — my rock, my biggest cheerleader, my safe place. Thank you for believing in me, grounding me, and giving me the space to write and reflect. I couldn't do this without you.

To my family and friends who walked with me during the seasons of writing, waiting, and rewriting — your prayers, support, and love carried me.

And above all, I give thanks to **God**, who teaches us that quiet faithfulness matters and that we don't need a spotlight to make a difference. May all who read this book be reminded that leading with peace, obedience, and trust is powerful in ways the world may never fully see — but heaven does.

Thank you for being part of this journey with me.

— **Myriam Muñiz**

About the Author

Myriam Muñiz is a leadership coach, writer, and speaker who believes that true influence often happens quietly, faithfully, and behind the scenes. After more than 30 years in corporate America, she transitioned into coaching to help individuals and emerging leaders discover their purpose and lead with integrity.

Born and raised in Spanish Harlem and now living in Florida with her husband and three dogs, Myriam draws inspiration from both her faith and her journey through seasons of change, uncertainty, and perseverance. She is the founder of **Momentum Moves Mountains**, a career and leadership development company, and the author of several works focused on faith-driven leadership and personal growth.

Myriam's heart is for the steady leaders—the ones who might not seek the spotlight but carry powerful, lasting influence. Her passion is to remind readers and clients alike: *you don't have to be loud to be legendary*.

When she's not writing or coaching, Myriam enjoys quiet mornings with a cup of tea, lively

"Godversations" with friends, and movie nights that often find their way into her writing.

Connect with Myriam:

- Website: www.myriamcmuniz.com

- Instagram: @myriamcmunizMMM

- LinkedIn: www.linkedin.com/in/myriam-muniz

Other Books
by Myriam Muñiz

Now What? A Journey to Future Career Success
Follow Sofia Esperanza as she embarks on a new beginning, exploring fresh career paths and personal growth. A motivating guide filled with practical strategies and faith-centered encouragement for anyone facing a transition.

Now What? Empowering Graduates on Their Career Journeys
Designed for college and trade school graduates, this book offers career advice, real-world tips, and inspiring stories to help young professionals navigate the early stages of their careers with confidence and purpose.

For more information about Myriam Muñiz and upcoming releases, visit www.myriamcmuniz.com